SCHOLASTIC'S A+ JUNIOR GUIDE TO GOOD WRITING

LOUISE COLLIGAN

SCHOLASTIC INC.
New York Toronto London Auckland Sydney

ISBN 0-590-40591-8

12 11 10 9 8 7 6 5 4 3   2 3/9

Printed in the U.S.A.   28

First Scholastic printing, January 1988

Table of Contents

1
Help, I've Got a Paper Due! What Do I Do First?

Remember the good old days when writing and penmanship meant the same thing? When your teacher put a smiley face on your paper just for writing your letters in a nice straight line? In the middle grades, you may be finding out that writing is a whole lot more than dotting your i's and crossing your t's. And that it's harder than ever to earn that smiley face.

Now that you are older, writing may seem pretty complicated. First, you're supposed to come up with a great idea for a paper. Or do something creative with a topic your teacher hands out to everyone. Then you are expected to organize the idea somehow. And, on top of all that, your paper is supposed to look really neat with every word spelled perfectly! Is it any wonder that a lot of middle school kids like you get discouraged in front of a piece of blank paper? And that a lot of you wait until the last minute to do your papers?

1

Is there a solution to all this? The answer is YES! *You* are the person who can solve most of your writing problems, and this book will show you how, step by step.

But first let's find the writer in you. Remember that you are a person with thoughts and feelings, friends and family, and perhaps even a pet or two; with likes and dislikes, interests and hobbies, dreams and plans. You have had experiences in your life that have made you laugh and cry. You have sometimes been brave — sometimes a little scared. Being a writer is being able to get at all of that and write about it.

This book will show how to organize your thoughts, how to write a good first sentence, how to develop a paragraph, how to revise and edit. But those steps aren't nearly as important as finding the real you to write about.

Kids your age often think they have to write about something big, something *out there*, and they often overlook their own lives as they look for subjects they think will impress the teacher. This search can make writing a lot harder than it has to be. To help convince you that some of the best writing topics come from real life, this book lists over a hundred writing topics — all of them designed to make the most of the experiences and interests of middle school students like you. You will find these topics on pages 94–101 of this book.

Now to answer the question every student writer worries about — What do I do first? Let's break down the big job of writing a paper into ten smaller jobs that even the most nervous writer can manage one by one. In later chapters, you will see just how to follow these steps for five different types of papers students in your grade are often asked to write.

Ten Steps to A+ Writing

Prewriting

Step 1: Get personal. Write about what you know or find a way to make an assigned topic more personal.

Step 2: Think small. Narrow your subject down to a workable size.

Step 3: Make a list. List all the specific ideas and details you can think of about your topic.

Step 4: Organize. Decide how you want to arrange the ideas and details on your list.

Writing

Step 5: Introduce. Write your opening sentence.

Step 6: Develop. Write supporting paragraphs that develop the main ideas from your planning list.

Step 7: Write your ending.

Step 8: Think of a title.

Revising and Editing

Step 9: Revise. Reread your paper to see if you can change or improve what you have written.

Step 10: Edit and recopy. Correct spelling, grammar, and punctuation. Recopy your corrected paper.

Does this sound like ten times more work than you do already? It's not if you work on a few steps at a time. A half hour a night for three nights should give you enough time to work on almost any kind of paper except a research report. Spend one night on the prewriting steps; write your rough draft on a second night; revise, edit, and recopy on a third night.

Now let's take the steps one by one and see how each one will lead you to a super paper.

Prewriting

Step 1: Get personal. Write about what you know or find a way to make an assigned topic more personal. What subject are you the number one expert on? You! Now maybe you think your life is too ordinary to write about. Wrong! Your life has high points (like the day your soccer team got into the playoffs) and low ones (like the time you had to go to the emergency room for stitches). If you find the right words, you can make a reader hungry (by describing your favorite meal), or giggly (by telling about the egg race you had at summer camp). You can educate your reader (by explaining how to make salt crystals or pitch a winning softball game). You can even bring your reader right into your life (by describing your room in detail), or introduce someone to your pet (by telling about the first day you got it). Your life is jam-packed with experiences if you know how to get at them.

Okay, you say to yourself, I guess I can think of a couple things in my life to write about that aren't too boring. But what if the teacher gives us a boring subject? Believe it or not, there are ways to take even the dullest subject and make it interesting just by putting a little of yourself into it.

Suppose your social studies teacher says: "I want you to write a paper about why people should vote." You feel a big yawn coming on, not to mention a feeling of dread. Since you don't vote, how are you supposed to make a subject like that more personal? Here are a couple of ideas. Why not interview people you know who *do* vote, like your parents or your next-door neighbors, and write about their opinions? Or write a paper on why you wish you *could* have voted in the last election. This is called "getting an angle" on your subject, and it's something you can do in your head.

Do you know what's worse than a boring assigned subject? When your teacher says you can write about anything at all. If that happens, see if you can find a good topic in the last chapter of this book.

Where else can you look for good ideas? Newspapers and weekly news magazines are good places. Many newspapers recently carried a great story about a mother who bet her ten-year-old son that he couldn't give up television for a year. How about a paper related to a real-life story like that? Just reading about lottery winners makes a lot of people think about what they would do if they won millions. The problems in advice columns can get you thinking about what you would do in the same spot.

Many writers keep diaries. If that appeals to you, try writing a little about yourself when you are in the mood. Write down interesting experiences, bits of conversations, weird ideas you get, interesting things you see, or impressions of the world around you. In your notebook collect photos, labels, ticket stubs, and odds and ends that might later trigger off something worth writing about.

Once you get in the habit of looking for ideas all over — from television, newspapers, magazines, daily life — you will find plenty of good writing subjects.

Step 2: Think small. Narrow your subject down to a workable size. Teachers usually try to assign topics that everyone can write about. As a result, their topics may be too big and too general. To make your writing job easier, you have to figure out a way to zero in on it.

The best kind of writing focuses in on the details of a subject — not your entire house but perhaps just your room; not your puppy but a day in the life of your puppy; not the whole circus but just the daring aerialist.

In writing, focusing on a small, interesting part of a big subject is similar to taking a picture. You see more details the closer you get to your subject.

Step 3: Make a list. List as many specific ideas and details as you can think of about your topic. You won't use them all, but the more you get down on paper, the easier the actual writing will be later on. Try to come up with specifics that will *show* rather than tell someone about your subject. If you've been asked to write about the Fourth of July, do your thoughts immediately revolve around your family's annual barbeque? Or do you think about the parade you march in every year? Maybe a trip your family made to the Liberty Bell in Philadelphia reminds you of the Fourth of July.

Be specific. Think "buttercups" not "flowers"; "polka-dotted dalmation" not "dog"; "puffball" rather than simply "kitten." Use your senses and memory to gather up good details. Put yourself right into the situation you are writing about. If your topic is your favorite beach, think about the waves that slap your back; the sand that burns the soles of your feet; the bright kites sailing the sky. In this way, you will make your paper so special that no one else could have written it.

Step 4: Organize. Decide on how you want to arrange your list of ideas and details. First, read over your list a few times. What do most of the details have in common? Try to think of an idea that would tie the details together. Suppose your subject is ice hockey, for example, and most of the details you listed have to do with equipment. Then you might be able to write a useful buyer's guide for someone interested in the sport. If your details seem to be about one exciting game, then a moment-by-moment description of the game would work out best.

Once you have an overall idea of what you want your paper to be about, you can arrange your list of details in several ways:

• You can number the details in the order you might want to use them. (Cross out any that don't fit in with your main idea.)

• You can group together the details that have something in common and arrange the groups in the order you will write about them.

• You can write an outline if your teacher requires one. There's a model for one on pages 82–84.

No matter how you organize your list, the thinking part is the same. Your list leads you to an overall idea of what you want to say about your subject. Then you group together details that tie in with your main idea. You will find examples of how to follow this thinking in the five kinds of sample papers included in this book.

Writing

Step 5: Introduce. Every piece of writing begins with one sentence. Do you find that first sentence the hardest of all to write? Most writers do when they realize how much they have to get across in that opener. The best opening sentences:

• catch the reader's attention right away so he or she will want to read more;

• introduce the reader to the subject;

• set the mood for the rest of the paper.

No wonder a lot of writers sit and stare, chew on their pencils, or suddenly clean out their desk drawers when faced with writing that all-important opener.

Here's a great piece of advice to keep in mind as you chew on your own pencil: "Tell 'em what you're going to say. Say it. Then tell 'em what you've said."

So what's the best way to "Tell 'em what you're going to say"? Here are some examples of openers that do just that:

Topic: How to equip yourself for ice hockey

Main idea: I want to tell someone interested in ice hockey what they'll need to buy.

Possible opening sentences:

Save your allowance or start mowing lawns if you want to get into ice hockey.

Don't spend any money on ice hockey equipment until you've read this paper!

Ice hockey can be expensive, but it's worth every nickel.

Topic: Sometimes a person outgrows a friend

Main idea: I want to show the reader how awful it feels to stop seeing a friend.

Possible opening sentences:

Losing a friend is like losing a piece of yourself.

Sometimes when I see a person with curly red hair, I think it's my old friend Robin.

Losing a good friend seems like the worst thing in the world, but it isn't.

Notice how each of these openers gets across the main idea right away and how the writer gets a certain mood across as well. A well-planned first sentence points you in the right direction for the rest of the paper.

Step 6: Develop. If you follow these steps, your supporting sentences and paragraphs should fall into place like the pieces of a puzzle.

Have your planning list of details in front of you

as you write the main part of your paper. Plan to write a paragraph for each group of details on your list or outline. Keep in mind that a paragraph is a group of sentences about one idea. Start a new paragraph each time you move on to a new idea. Use linking words like those shown on pages 41 and 42 to connect the paragraphs.

Step 7: Write your last sentence. "Tell 'em what you've said." The best way to sum up your paper is to get that same feeling in your last sentence as you got across in your first. If you started funny, end funny. If you've been trying to teach or persuade your reader, write a sentence that repeats, in a new way, the point of your opener.

Here are some pairs of sentences. The first is an opener; the second, an ending. Notice how each one mirrors the other:

First sentence: *Thud!* The morning paper hits the driveway, and Bellwood Avenue is awake.

Last sentence: As I drift off to sleep, I know the next sound I will hear on Bellwood Avenue will be: *Thud!*

First sentence: Sometimes when I see a person with curly red hair, I think it's my old friend Robin.

Last sentence: There are other kids with curly hair and other redheads, too, but my old friend Robin was one-of-a-kind.

First sentence: Save your allowance or start mowing lawns if you want to get into ice hockey.

Last sentence: There are less expensive sports you can get into, but none of them has the excitement and speed that make ice hockey worth the cost.

Step 8: Think of a title. Although the title introduces your paper, work on it last. Why? Once you have a rough draft, you will have already worked out your subject, details, main idea, style, and tone. Your title should get across some of that.

Your title can sum up your material in a matter-of-fact way. It can tease the reader a little. Or make the reader smile in anticipation.

Here are some titles that get across the subjects listed and capture some of the feeling a writer might want to share:

Subject: The toughest basketball game I ever played
Title: *Foul Play!*
Subject: What happens when you lose a friend
Title: *Going Separate Ways*
Subject: Equipping yourself for ice hockey
Title: *A Buyer's Guide for New Hockey Players*

Revise and Edit

Step 9: Revise. Have you ever gotten a corrected paper back from your teacher and wished you'd had one last chance to copy your paper over? If you get in the habit of revising rough drafts, *you* can make those colored markings before the teacher does. Revising means changing your paper to make it even better. Here is how to go about it.

Gather together a colored pencil as well as a dictionary and thesaurus, if you have them. Then turn to the Revising Sheet on pages 86 and 87. Ask yourself the questions listed there as you read through your paper.

To make changes, use the Proofreading Sheet on page 88. These special markings show you how to add new words, take out old ones, and switch around sentences and paragraphs.

Now move on to:

Step 10: Edit and recopy. Your first draft probably looks like something your dog wrote at this point — full of weird markings and words stuck in, erased, or crossed out. Hang in there. Underneath all that is a pretty good paper if you have completed Steps 1–9. But "pretty good" isn't the same as "terrific," any more than a C or B is the same as an A.

Now that you have completed your revision — fixing your organization, style, and wording — read through your rough draft one last time. Check that spelling, punctuation, and grammar are correct. Follow the Editing Sheet on page 87 as a guide for making corrections. If you need to check simple grammar rules, turn to pages 89–93. Use a dictionary to check on spelling you are not sure about.

Once you have made your final changes, get some clean paper. Put your name, date, and the name of your class at the top, and slowly recopy your rough draft.

Now take your paper, put it into your bookbag, and go treat yourself to a snack, a television program, or an activity you've been looking forward to.

If you have completed most of these steps, you are going to turn in the best possible paper. And remember, if you don't have a writing folder at school, keep one at home to collect your work. You might want to read over recent papers just before your next writing assignment. On your next paper, do more of what your teacher liked; less of what he or she disliked.

The next several chapters show you exactly how to follow the writer's ten-step plan for just the kinds of papers middle schoolers like you are often assigned — a personal narrative, a description, a how-to paper, a paper in which the writer tries to persuade a reader about a personal opinion, and a research report.

2
What's the Story?
Writing a Personal Narrative

It is mid-September but still hot enough to feel like summer. Instead of sitting by a pool drinking lemonade, you are in English class. Instead of wearing a bathing suit, which would be a lot more comfortable, you are hot and itchy in your new school clothes. Instead of doing a cannonball off the high-dive, you are sitting in front of your brand-new empty notebook all ready to jot down the first big writing assignment of this school year.

"One of the ways I like to find out about my new students," your teacher begins, "is to read about what they did over the summer." You hear a few groans around the room. Like the groaners, you know what's coming next. "So class, by this Friday, I would like you to write a paper about how you spent your summer vacation."

More groans. Part of you wishes your family had taken you on a raft trip to the Grand Canyon or on an African safari instead of to Indian Lake. The other part of you wonders if you still have the other two papers you wrote a couple of years back on this same boring subject. Not likely, since your old papers usually wind up crumpled in the bottom of your locker, then thrown out.

Even though your summer vacation just ended, you can hardly remember where the two months went. Except for a couple of weeks at Indian Lake, it seems as if all you did was hang out. Not much there to write about. You're pretty sure this new teacher isn't going to want to hear about how you got up at ten o'clock every day or how many reruns you watched on TV.

Your teacher continues: "I see a few frowns around the room. To make this easier on you, I want you to think of this topic as a kind of story. What you will be writing is something called a *personal narrative*. That means telling a story about something that happened to you."

A couple of hands go up.

"How long is the paper supposed to be?" one voice whines.

"Short enough so no one gets bored reading it; long enough to tell your story," the teacher answers.

How come, you wonder, teachers hardly ever tell you exactly how long they want a paper to be?

You always guess around three pages, but you are never sure whether your paper is too short or too long.

"Are we supposed to use ink or pencil?" someone else wants to know.

"Your first draft can be in pencil, but your final paper should be in ink or typed."

That isn't what you wanted to hear. Now you know. You'll have to write two papers — a sloppy one and a clean one. That's what "draft" means to you — twice the work. Right about now, you just know the entire class would probably vote for a thousand-word spelling test instead of this paper. Unfortunately, the teacher isn't leaving it up to a vote; she's busy writing down the due date, which is five days away.

The bell rings, freeing you from any more miserable thoughts about this writing assignment. You've got plenty of time, five days, right? You just erase the whole thing from your mind for now.

Shift to Thursday night, the night before the due date of your paper. What have you written so far about your summer vacation? You check your assignment pad again. Maybe she meant *next* Friday. No chance. You did write something down — the topic, the due date, and "narrative," which you can't quite remember the meaning of. The whole assignment seems sort of hazy, and you can't believe how fast those five days flew by.

Then you check your big notebook, and there it is, what you were avoiding all week, A BLANK SHEET OF PAPER! You're sick, and your neck aches. Maybe you're getting the flu and should go to bed immediately. But tomorrow, besides being D-Day for this paper, is also the first day of fall soccer practice. If you get sick enough to miss school, there goes your soccer career. Looks like you have no choice but to write that paper. But how?

Here's how you might go about doing a narrative paper on how you spent your summer vacation. First, get yourself situated in your best thinking and working spot, away from television, your little sister, and your barking dog. Make sure you have a couple of sharp pencils with erasers, a colored pen or pencil for corrections, and a ballpoint for your final copy if that's what your teacher requires. Use scrap paper for your rough draft and better paper for your final copy. If you have a dictionary and thesaurus, keep them nearby. They'll be a big help when you want to check spelling or find certain words. You might also want to clip the revising, editing, and proofreading pages in the back of this book when you check over your rough draft.

Now tell yourself that for the next hour or so, you are going to work on this paper and do nothing else. If your mind wanders to the refrigerator or television, decide that when your paper is done you are going to give yourself a treat. Here goes.

Assignment: "Write a paper about your summer vacation."

Prewriting

Step 1: Get personal. Luckily your assigned subject, "How I Spent My Summer Vacation," is already about something personal. So why do you dread writing about it? Because suddenly your summer seems kind of dull. On top of that, you can hardly remember what happened a couple of weeks ago, let alone way back in July. You sit there looking at all your writing materials and wonder how you'll get a paper from all of it.

Move on to:

Step 2: Think small. The problem with "How I Spent My Summer Vacation" isn't that your summer was dull. It's that this topic is way too big to write about. Now it's time to think of a way to bring it down to a size you can handle.

Either in your head, but preferably on scrap paper, list a few parts of the summer that you do remember as being a little different than the average summer day — experiences you could tell about in a real-life story. Here is a sample list of narrowed-down topics:

- Arriving at Indian Lake
- Comparing a typical summer day to a school day
- The day you saw a toddler fall into the baby pool and you picked her up before the mother even knew the baby had fallen in
- The night you camped out in your backyard with just your friends

Even the most discouraged writers would start to feel more confident with a list like this. Not only are these narrower topics a lot more personal, but each one will probably trigger lots of memories to write about.

From this list of smaller topics, a writer would pick just one to write about. Let's imagine you chose the one about fishing that toddler out of the baby pool.

Now move on to:

Step 3: Make a list. Gathering a list of specific details is one of the best ways to zoom in on your subject. This is the time to use your senses. What do you *see* in your mind? What do you *hear, taste, smell, feel?*

Write all these things down as they pop into your head. You probably won't use everything you write down, but one good detail, one good idea, leads to another.

Here is what a list of details about this subject might look like:

- big white clock with black hands over baby pool
- lying on the pool deck to warm up after being in the pool
- smells: damp smell of chlorine; smell of hamburgers half-burning at snack bar
- sounds: hum of people talking, kids laughing, ear-splitting lifeguard whistle; mothers telling kids they can't have potato chips before lunch
- half asleep
- wet feet slapping on deck
- thinking about what to have for lunch
- toddler pool
- clock-watching; saw baby topple while mother's head was turned
- scraped my foot
- picked baby up — coughing, crying, dripping
- thank you over and over — mother
- embarrassment

A list something like this would help you relive the experience so that you could write about it.

Step 4: Organize. No problem here. The logical way to organize a personal narrative is to follow an experience moment by moment.

Some teachers prefer that you organize your details into an outline like this one:

I. Setting
  A. Lying on the beach towel
    1. relaxed but hungry
    2. too lazy to get up
  B. Everyday pool sounds around me
    1. hum of voices and shrieking
    2. splashing
    3. lifeguard whistle
    4. wet feet slapping on deck
  C. Smells
    1. chlorine on hot cement
    2. burning hamburgers
  D. Sights
    1. black-and-white pool clock
    2. toddler pool
II. What happened
  A. Checked time
  B. Baby toppled
  C. Hard to decide what to do
  D. Scraped my foot on cement deck
  E. Leaped up and scooped baby
III. Afterwards
  A. Crying baby coughing and dripping
  B. Mother thanking me
  C. Embarrassment

This list is arranged in an outline, and you will find a model for one on pages 82–84. But most writers usually group related ideas together. For a personal narrative, one logical way to group the details would be under the headings *beginning, middle, end*. Or simply number the details in the order you would want to use them.

Once you have an idea of the order you will follow in your paper, you are ready to move on to:

Writing

Step 5: Introduce. To come up with a first sentence, ask yourself, "What do I want to get across to the reader in this paper?" Some possible answers might be something like:

"I want to show how just two minutes of my summer vacation stood out from the rest of the two months."

Or: "I want to get across how even when you're doing nothing, something unexpected can happen fast."

Most of all, you probably want to make sure your teacher sees right away that you did the assignment called for. With all that in mind, here are some sample first lines for the paper:

• "It was an ordinary summer day at the pool, just like all the ones before it and the ones that came afterward."

• "My summer vacation lasted over two months, but what I remember the most are two of the longest minutes I ever had."

• "One ordinary summer day, I was lying in the sun and trying to decide about lunch, and a minute later I saved a baby's life."

Step 6: Develop. You are now ready to turn some of the items on your planning list into sentences and group those sentences into paragraphs. Here's a rough draft of the paper, which also shows the revisions and corrections that would be made in Steps 9 and 10.

One minute of ~~a typical~~ an ordinary summer day, I was

lying in the sun and trying to decide about

lunch, and a minute later I saved a baby's life. I

don't even remember what day it was, but ~~I do~~

~~know~~ I was doing what I always did on most of

my summer days. I was trying to get a the perfect suntan.

~~Lieing~~ Lying on my towel, I listened to the usual

sounds of summer, like the lifeguard's whistle,

feet slapping by on the wet deck, and radios playing.

Over the smell of chlorine came the smell of burning hamburgers, the kind you can only eat with a gallon of ketchup. I was hungry, but I was too lazy to lift my body from the deck. I looked up and checked the time on the pool's big white clock. The black hands pointed only to 11:30. It was too early for lunch.

Then, as I lowered my head back to my towel, I saw a baby Topple to from where she was sitting in the water. She was underwater, but right away I could see no one had noticed. The person closest to her, probably the mother, was watching another child. For some reason, I remembered something I'd been told from my babysitting course. A baby can drown in an inch of water.

I got up from my towel, scraping my toes against the concrete, and ran to that baby. She was

25

staring straight up from under the water and

didn't even look su~~r~~prised. Everything seemed to

move ~~slowly~~ *in slow motion*.

I got her out of the water. She was dripping,

coughing, and crying at the same time. The

mother took her and kept thanking me over and

over.

Everybody was watching as I stood there *like a post*. "It's

okay," I ~~said~~ *mumbled*.

All this paper needs now is a sentence to tie
everything up, so move on to:

Step 7: Write your ending. Sometimes, a good last
line comes to you as you write. Other times you
have to work at it. Ask yourself if the last line you
wrote brings the reader back to the setting and
feeling of the first line.

Since the writer opens by describing an ordinary
setting, how about echoing back to that at the end?
Here are a couple of possibilities for tying up this
paper neatly:

• "Suddenly I was starving."
• "It was time for that hamburger."

Step 8: Think of a title. The title is the icing on the cake. If you have completed all the steps so far, doesn't your paper deserve a catchy name? Here are two that tie in with the assignment:

- *Junior Lifesaving*
- *How I Spent Two Minutes of My Summer Vacation*

If you have used up all your brainpower on your paper and can't think of another thing, how about: *How I Spent My Summer Vacation*? After all, that's what your teacher called the assignment, so you know she'll go for that title.

Now move on to:

Revising and Editing

Step 9: Revise. The first draft is done. Take a breather before you begin to revise. Most writers find they can judge their work better if they put it aside to "cool" for a while. If you're a real plan-ahead person, you might want to save this step for the last night. Like many writers, though, you may be working on your paper right before it's due. In that case, you'll only have time to set aside your paper for a half hour or so. Go do something totally unrelated to writing for that half hour.

Once you're back, get your colored pencil or marker ready, your dictionary and thesaurus, and open this book to the Revising Sheet on pages 86 and 87 and the Proofreading Sheet on page 88 (put a clip on those pages, so you can flip to them quickly).

On your first reading of the rough draft, ask yourself the questions about organization and style. This is the time to switch around sentences, put in new words, and take out those that don't work. You can see from the rough draft above how improvements were made.

Step 10: Edit and recopy. Reread the paper one more time, this time checking for spelling, punctuation, and grammar mistakes. Make the corrections, then recopy your paper neatly. Here's what a final draft of this particular paper would look like:

<u>How I Spent Two Minutes of My Summer</u>
<u>Vacation</u>

One minute of an ordinary summer day, I was lying in the sun and trying to decide about lunch, and a minute later I saved a baby's life. I don't even remember what day it was, but I was doing what I always did on most of my summer days. I was trying to get the perfect suntan.

Lying on my towel, I listened to the usual sounds of summer, like the lifeguard's whistle, feet slapping by on the wet deck, and radios playing.

Over the smell of chlorine came the smell of

burning hamburgers, the kind you can only eat with a gallon of ketchup. I was hungry, but I was too lazy to lift my body from the deck. I looked up and checked the time on the pool's big white clock. The black hands pointed only to 11:30. It was too early for lunch.

Then, as I lowered my head back to my towel, I saw a baby topple from where she was sitting into the water. She was underwater, but right away I could see no one had noticed. The person closest to her, probably the mother, was watching another child. For some reason, I remembered something I'd been told from my baby-sitting course. A baby can drown in an inch of water.

I got up from my towel, scraping my toes against the concrete, and ran to that baby. She was staring straight up from under the water and didn't even look surprised. Everything seemed to move in slow motion.

I got her out of the water. She was dripping, coughing, and crying at the same time. The mother took her and kept thanking me over and over.

Everybody was watching as I stood there like a post. "It's okay," I mumbled.

Suddenly I was starving.

3
Come to Your Senses: Writing a Description

Writing is a way of sharing your world with other people. The ways in which you see, hear, smell, taste, and feel are special to you. When you want to share your world with a reader, you need to find the words that will make your reader see what you saw, hear what you heard, experience what you smelled, tasted, and felt.

One way to do this is by using very specific words. For example:

- "crashing waves" rather than "stormy ocean"
- "old gym socks" rather than "musty"
- "bubbling apple pie" rather than "dessert"
- "pebbly" rather than "rough"
- "shuffled" rather than "walked slowly"
- "gobbled" rather than "ate quickly"

Similes are a good way to make comparisons between something from ordinary life and something imaginary. For example:

- "ears that looked like small pink seashells"

- "a sky that looked like silver glitter on black velvet"
- "a sound that split the air like a thunderclap"

Mark Twain once said, "The difference between the right word and the nearly right word is the same as that between lightning and the lightning bug." A dictionary-style thesaurus is just the place to track down the word you really want to use instead of settling for the nearly right word. Here are some examples of good word choices you could find in a thesaurus:

- fog: mist, vapor, haze, cloud
- jump: hop, leap, bound, spring, vault
- wet: damp, moist, dewy, clammy, dank, humid
- walk: stroll, ramble, saunter, hike, march

With a thesaurus on hand as you write, you will not only locate the perfect word, but you will build up your vocabulary as well.

Keep in mind that the key to writing good descriptions is using your five senses to think of the most specific words possible. Now let's see how to use the ten writing steps to come up with the kind of vivid description a middle schooler would be proud to turn in.

Let's say the assignment is this: *"Write a description of a special place you've been to."* How would you begin? First, write down the due date. Find out if you have to turn in lists, outlines, and a rough draft along with the final paper. Then plan a work schedule so that you don't wind up doing the whole paper in one night. This three-part plan would work well for most student writers: one night for prewriting, one for writing the rough draft, and a final night for revising, editing, and recopying. A plan like this would give you plenty of time for other homework and some free time besides.

Prewriting

Step 1: Get personal. Luckily, this is another assignment that you can tie in to your own life. What place would you most like to share with someone? Let's say you decide on your grandmother's house. Now move on to:

Step 2: Think small. You picked your grandmother's house as a subject because it's a huge old place full of nooks and crannies to explore, a wraparound gingerbread porch, loads of rooms, and a big yard. Now, how are you going to get all that down on paper? You're not! Instead, start thinking of a part of her house, not all of it. What about the attic, where you spent hours of your childhood playing with old toys? Or how about describing that big old kitchen? Or the cedar closet full of wonderful old clothes? Maybe the smells you associate with the house are part of what makes the place special — lilacs in the spring, lemon polish on the furniture, roast chicken on Sundays.

Here's a possible list of smaller subjects to consider:

- the attic on a rainy day
- the kitchen right before Christmas
- the old porch
- the cedar closet hideout
- the different smells of Grandma's house

Let's say you decide on the cedar closet hiding place at your grandmother's.

Now move on to:

Step 3: Make a list. Close your eyes and imagine yourself at your grandmother's house on a Sunday afternoon right after a big dinner. You and a couple of cousins are playing your favorite game — hide-and-seek.

On a piece of paper, list some of the details you remember about your favorite hideout. What would someone see, hear, smell, feel, or taste there? Here's what a planning list might look like:

Grown-ups in dining room
restless kids

Home base:
hall under the stairs
little shelf for old black telephone

Cedar closet:
forest smell
hatboxes
fire fighter's hat
all kinds of shoes in old boxes
beaded dresses
I would forget I was hiding
feelings I had then and now

Step 4: Organize. These details are already arranged in the same time order as they took place. So unless the teacher requires an outline, the writer could move on to:

Writing

Step 5: Introduce. To come up with an opening sentence, ask yourself what you want the reader to experience. Do you want your reader to see the house from a child's point of view as you saw it? With this in mind, here are a couple of possibilities that would introduce the reader to this special place:

• "My grandmother's house is full of places you could get lost in."

• "Imagine a house where you could get lost and not get found for a long time."

• "Playing hide-and-seek at my grandmother's was like getting lost in a time machine."

Step 6: Develop. Now you are ready to go through your planning list and write paragraphs for each group of details. You may find yourself adding details or crossing out others. The list is really meant to get you thinking about very specific memories.

Here is a rough draft of the paper:

My grandmother's house was full of places you could get lost in. My cousins and I played games of hide-and-seek there while the grown-ups talked about boring things ^like whether the gravy was too lumpy

Hide-and-seek always began in the downstairs hall by the stairs. The ⌐heavy old black phone was on a little shelf ~~cut~~ carved right into the wall. If you were "it," you put your head down on that shelf, closed your eyes, and began counting while everyone else scattered ~~ran off.~~

One favorite hiding place was Grandma's cedar closet, just off the attic. It always smelled like a forest when I went in there. When my grandfather was alive, he sanded it down every spring

to make the cedar give off that smell.

My grandmother stored clothes in there, like old

beaded dresses and soft blouses in all colors. There were dusty hatboxes stacked

on the shelves. If I wasn't found right away, I

tried on some of my grandparents' hats. Along

with Grandma's many hats was my grand-

father's heavy fire fighter helmet, which he had worn

when he was a volunteer.

Off in one corner was a pile of shoe boxes

from stores that probably don't exist anymore.

The shoes inside were still wrapped in layers of tissue as

if they were brand-new. There were shoes with

rhinestone clips, silk shoes, even a pair almost

like the ones Dorothy wore in <u>The Wizard of Oz.</u>

When I was hiding out in the cedar closet, I

sometimes forgot everything outside that little

room. But I will never forget the room itself.

Step 7: Write your ending. Now go back to the beginning sentence again. What is the main point you made? What's the mood? Here are some last sentences that echo back to the first one:

- "I would love to go back there and lose myself in the cedar closet just one last time."
- "I've never found a house that was better for getting lost in than my grandmother's."
- "I must have played hide-and-seek a hundred times in all sorts of places, but my grandmother's house was the only one where I never wanted to be found."

Step 8: Think of a title. Like your first and last sentences, a title should make your reader want to read on. A good title should tease the reader a little, yet not mislead. Here are some choices:

- *Hideout*
- *Lost and Found*
- *Hide-and-Seek*

Revise and Edit

Step 9: Revise. As you look over the rough draft, notice how many specific adjectives were added to help the reader really *sense* what the writer sensed. Details like this bring a subject to life for the reader.

Notice how the writer works at finding just the right word: "carved" instead of "cut," "scattered" in place of "ran off,""helmet" instead of "hat."

Step 10: Edit and recopy. As you can see from the rough draft, the writer corrected spelling, punctuation, and grammar mistakes. On your own papers, take that extra last step to reread your paper slowly, word for word. Catch those mistakes before your teacher does.

When you are satisfied that you have fixed everything possible, recopy the paper. Here is what the final draft of the description looks like:

Lost and Found

My grandmother's house was full of places you could get lost in. My cousins and I played games of hide-and-seek there while the grown-ups talked about boring things, like whether the gravy was too lumpy.

Hide-and-seek always began in the downstairs hall by the stairs. The heavy old black phone was on a little shelf carved right into the wall. If you were "it," you put your head down on that shelf, closed your eyes, and began counting while everyone else scattered.

One favorite hiding place was Grandma's cedar closet, just off the attic. It always smelled like a forest when I went in there. When my grandfather was alive, he sanded it down every spring to make the cedar give off that smell.

My grandmother stored clothes in there, like

old beaded dresses and soft blouses in all colors. There were dusty hatboxes stacked on the shelves. If I wasn't found right away, I tried on some of my grandparents' hats. Along with Grandma's many hats was my grandfather's heavy fire fighter helmet, which he had worn when he was a volunteer.

Off in one corner was a pile of shoe boxes from stores that probably don't exist anymore. The shoes inside were still wrapped in layers of tissue as if they were brand-new. There were shoes with rhinestone clips, silk shoes, even a pair almost like the ones Dorothy wore in The Wizard of Oz.

When I was hiding out in the cedar closet, I sometimes forgot everything outside that little room. But I will never forget the room itself. I would love to go back there and lose myself in the cedar closet just one last time.

4
Explain That!
Writing a How-to Paper

Have you ever tried to put together one of those birthday presents that comes with a bag of nuts, bolts, screws, and a set of instructions that seem to be written in a foreign language? Or cooked up a pan of fudge that didn't harden, even though you followed the recipe? If so, then you know how tricky following directions can be.

Writing clear directions is even trickier. One well-known writing exercise asks new writers to come up with directions for making a peanut butter sandwich. Sounds simple, doesn't it? Do you know that when students try to follow each other's directions, most of the kids never even get the lid off the jar? This happens because most writers forget to mention that you have to hold down the peanut butter jar with one hand while unscrewing the lid with the other!

Explaining a process step-by-step is one kind of *expository writing*. As you get into the older grades, you will be asked to explain many subjects: how certain government groups work; how to do a science experiment; how to work out a math problem. But no matter what the subject is, writers of clear directions:

• tell right away what they are going to explain.

• list all the materials someone would need ahead of time.

• explain each step in the same time order in which it takes place.

• use verbs that tell what action to take.

• connect steps with *linking* words like these:

To show time:

first, second, etc.	next	later
to begin with	moreover	finally
begin by	soon	to sum up
start with/by	in addition	in conclusion
at the beginning	after that	
in the first place	furthermore	
	besides	
	another	
	then (avoid overuse)	
	in the second/next place	
	meanwhile	
	in addition	
	not long after	
	also (avoid overuse)	

To show results:

therefore	consequently	as a result
thus	hence	

To show contrast:

on the contrary	on the other hand	nevertheless
however	instead	in spite of this

To show relationships:
similarly   likewise   accordingly
To give examples:
for example   for instance   an example of

Now let's take a look at how some of this advice would work out in the kind of how-to writing assignment you might get in the middle grades. A teacher might ask you to write a how-to paper explaining something simple, like taking care of a pet, getting into a sport, or doing a hobby. Here is a step-by-step example of how to handle this kind of writing assignment.

Assignment: "Write a paper explaining how to do something you are interested in."

Prewriting
Step 1: Get personal. Think about something you enjoy doing. It can be a sport, hobby, or just an everyday habit, like taking care of your gerbils. Let's say one of your favorite pastimes is magic, something that might be fun to write about.

Now move on to:
Step 2: Think small. Maybe you know dozens of magic tricks and have a large collection of trick items. But since your teacher asked for a simple how-to paper, your best bet is to focus on one trick any beginner could do, let's say your famous "Money Grows on Trees" trick.

Step 3: Make a list and *Step 4: Organize.* Explaining something start to finish is the best way to organize any how-to paper. So make up your list of details in the same order in which you will use them. Here's what a planning list for this topic might look like:

Introduction: magician's secrets
  give someone confidence

Materials needed:
  a couple of oranges
  glue
  a nickel
  a knife

Steps:
  paste a coin to knife ahead of time
  say that "money grows on trees" (or joke)
  slice into orange
  slide coin off knife while slicing fruit
  wind-up

Look over your list and steps. Have you included everything? If so, move on to:

Writing
Step 5: Introduce. Directions don't have to be dull. Try to get your readers' attention right off the bat.

Here are some possible openers for the magic trick topic:

- "Magicians never reveal their secrets, but this time I will make an exception."
- "Who says money doesn't grow on trees?"
- "A magic diet of oranges could make you healthy *and* rich at the same time."

Now move on to:

Step 6: Develop. Go through your list and write a sentence for each detail you included. But don't be afraid to add new information if you think of it.

Group the sentences into paragraphs: one paragraph to introduce your subject, a second paragraph of background information about magic, then a paragraph for each step. Here is a rough draft:

Magicians never reveal their secrets, but this time I will make an exception.

The first thing anyone should know about magic is that the magician only lets you see what he or she wants you to see. The magician makes you think what he or she wants you to think. So get everything ready ahead of time. Practice any new trick a couple of times alone so you can rehearse what you want to show.

For the "Money Grows on Trees" trick you will need:

glue

a nickle

dull
a knife

a couple of oranges.

Before you do the trick for anyone, ~~make sure~~ ~~to~~ glue the nickel to the knife blade. Keep the coin side of the blade toward you and away from the audience. Cut one of the oranges in half. Squeeze the two orange halves hard enough to push the nickel off. ~~Make sure to~~ try this a couple of times on your own until you get it right.

When you are ready to do the trick in ~~front of~~ public ~~someone,~~ pick up the uncut orange and the knife with the nickel glued on it. Show the audience

45

the ^whole orange and the knife. Say something like,
"Now I will show you that money grows on trees. This orange comes from a special tree I planted with nickels. Each of the oranges grew a nickel inside it. Take a look." (Hold up the orange.) I will now cut into the orange so you can see the nickel that grew inside."

Now, cut into the orange and squeeze the nickel off the knife as you cut through.

For your finish, hold up the orange ^halves showing the nickel and say, "Ta dah! or "Presto! or or something like that.

If anyone asks how you did the trick, you simply ~~say~~ just answer: "A magician never reveals his secrets."

Step 7: Write your ending. Notice that the last sentence is the same as part of the first sentence. This is a great way to wind up this paper.

Now move on to:

Step 8: Think of a title. Catch your readers' interest by:

- making them curious — *How to Make Money Grow on Trees*
- asking a question — *Do You Believe in Magic?*
- making them feel like insiders — *A Magician Reveals His Secrets*
- making them laugh — *Put Your Money Where Your Mouth Is*
- telling them what your paper is about — *How to Do a Magic Trick*

Revise and Edit

Step 9: Revise. Notice how much clearer the directions are when the writer begins a sentence with direct action verbs: "glue," "cut," "take," "show." Words like these make it easier for the reader to follow the steps.

See how the writer crossed out unnecessary words. Keep it simple when you write a how-to paper.

Step 10: Edit and recopy. Notice how the writer moved some sentences into new paragraphs. In a how-to paper, each step should have its own paragraph. Here is the final paper:

Magicians never reveal their secrets, but this time I will make an exception.

The first thing anyone should know about magic is that the magician only lets you see what he or she wants you to see. The magician makes you think what he or she wants you to think. So get everything ready ahead of time. Practice any new trick a couple of times alone so you can rehearse what you want to show.

For the "Money Grows on Trees" trick you will need:

glue

a nickel

a dull knife

a couple of oranges.

Before you do the trick for anyone, glue the nickel to the knife blade. Keep the coin side of the blade toward you and away from the audience.

Cut one of the oranges in half. Squeeze the two orange halves hard enough to push the nickel off as you cut. Try this a couple of times on your own until you get it right.

When you are ready to do the trick in public, pick up the uncut orange and the knife with the nickel glued on it. Show the audience the whole orange and the knife. Say something like, "Now I will show you that money grows on trees. This orange comes from a special tree I planted with nickels. Each of the oranges grew a nickel inside it. Take a look." (Hold up the orange.) "I will now cut into the orange so you can see the nickel that grew inside."

Now, cut into the orange and squeeze the nickel off the knife as you cut through.

For your finish, hold up the orange halves showing the nickel and say, "Ta dah!" or "Presto!" If anyone asks how you did the trick, just answer: "A magician never reveals his secrets."

5
Opinions, Opinions: Writing a Persuasive Paper

Do you think your allowance should be raised? Or that kids in your school ought to be allowed to have lunch off the school grounds? Can you think of five good reasons why kids your age ought to decide their own bedtimes? Above all, do you wish you were better at getting people to see things your way?

Persuasive writing is one of the best ways to learn how to argue logically. This skill is as useful in real life as it is in writing. Whether you are arguing at home about curfews or writing a school paper on why each homeroom should have two student council representatives, the thinking and planning skills are the same:

• You have to be convinced that you are right.

• You have to gather facts or reasons to prove you are right.

• You must organize your arguments in a clear way.

• You must figure out your opponent's (or reader's) arguments ahead of time and turn them to your advantage.

Now let's take a look at how you might put together a persuasive opinion paper on the kind of topic many students your age are asked to write about.

Assignment: "Write a paper trying to convince someone to change a family or school rule you disagree with."

Prewriting

Step 1: Get personal. Let's assume that what's bugging you most these days is your school's rule that students must spend their free periods in study hall or the library. Maybe this gets you and lots of other kids worked up because free periods are the only times you have to see your school friends. Since you have a personal opinion about this, move on to:

Step 2: Think small. You have already narrowed down the teacher's general assignment to something you can relate to, so go straight to:

Step 3: Make a list. You can easily think of what's wrong with your school's free-period system. And maybe you even have a few ideas of your own for improving things. If so, you would then list examples of both sides on a list like the following:

- kids get tired of sitting all day
- kids would get more independent if they could plan their own time
- try out free period for a month
- kids would pay more attention to later classes after a break
- study halls are too noisy
- too much planning of kids' time
- one free period a week
- kids who live far away could see each other
- not fair to kids who work best at home
- let B + and above students decide how to spend free periods

Step 4: Get organized. There are several ways you could organize the evidence you have gathered to support your point. Here are some of them:

Analyze: Look at the present free-period situation, take it apart, and show why it doesn't work.

Compare/Contrast: Describe the current situation, then show how much better your alternative would be.

Criticize: Give your opinion about the current situation and show its good and bad points.

Define: Explain what "free period" means to you.

Discuss: Present different points of view about the free-period issue and go over the pros and cons.

List: In order of their importance, list reasons why you think the present system should be changed.

Prove: Use specific examples to explain why the current system doesn't work.

How do you decide the best way to organize your paper? Go back to the planning list. Most of the details show the faults of the present system compared with the advantages of your system. So a *compare/contrast* plan would be a good way to arrange the ideas and examples. (If your teacher wants you to turn in an outline, use the model on pages 82–84 to group the details.)

Problems with present system:
too much planning of kids' time
kids get tired sitting all day
study halls noisy
not fair to kids who work best at home

Reasons for changing:
kids who live far away could see each other
kids would pay more attention to later classes after
    a break
kids would get more independent if they could
    plan their own time

Suggestions:
let B+ and above students decide how to spend
  free periods
try out for one month one really free period a week

Result:
kids more independent

Writing

Step 5: Introduce. Think about what you would
like your paper to do. "I want to convince someone
that middle school students are old enough to
choose what they want to do during free periods."
Or: "I want to persuade someone that there's a
better way for kids to use free periods."

Since your planning list is organized to compare
the old free-period system to a new, better one,
your opener should show that. Consider the following:

• "One of the best ways for kids to learn how to
use free time is by having free time to use."
• "What is free about free periods? Not too
much."
• "Every now and then it's a good idea to look
at the old ways of doing things and see if they can
be improved."
All of these openers would make a good introduction to the points you've listed for your paper.

Now see how one of them could be expanded by moving on to:

Step 6: Develop. Here is a rough draft of a paper comparing the disadvantages of the old system with the advantages of a new one:

One of the best ways to learn how to use free time is to have free time to use. At our school, every minute of a student's day is planned out from homeroom to ~~going home~~ dismissal. The free period isn't free at all since students have to go to study hall or the library during that time.

This is a bad plan. First of all, Most kids have been sitting in classes for a few periods before the free period comes up. They need to relax instead of sitting down ~~some more~~ again.

Second, The study halls are noisy. So even the kids who want to work get distracted by the noise of kids fooling around. On top of that, the study hall monitors spend most of their time yelling at kids to settle down.

~~Then~~ Finally, there's the library. Yes, it's quiet there

if you want to work, but is that the best time to

get work done? Maybe for some kids it is. But

what about kids who ~~like~~ prefer to do homework at

home? ~~We~~ They don't need ~~the time in~~ school to do

their homework.

There are some good reasons to change the

present free period to a better ~~plan~~ plan. ~~A~~ To begin with, a lot of kids

live to~~o~~ far away to see each other ~~accept~~ except at

school. Kids would pay better attention to their

later classes if they had a chance to relax before

~~then. Also~~ hand Most important, there's no better way for kids to learn

how to plan their free time than by giving them

a little of it.

~~The~~ Maybe people in charge will say that the present

plan helps kids who wouldn't do their home-

work ~~accept~~ except at school. Even if this is true, is it fair to most of the kids who get there homework done at home?

The school should try out different plans to see how they work. Maybe just kids with a B+ average or above could get real free periods. Or maybe everyone could get free periods for a month and see what happens. Even one really free period a week would be better than what we have now.

Step 7: Write your ending. Now go back to your opener and see how you can get that same opinion across in a new way. Here's a possibility:

"Everybody always says you learn from experience. So give students experience in planning their own free periods."

Step 8: Think of a title. In a persuasive opinion paper, the title should really get across your opinion right away. Here are some examples for this paper:

- *What's Free About Free Periods in Our School?*
- *How to Free Up Free Periods*

Revise and Edit

Step 9: Revise. Reread the rough draft. Notice how the writer introduced reasons for both sides with: "To begin with," "Second," "Most of all." Words like this draw attention to the writer's most important points.

Step 10: Edit and recopy. Read the final copy below. The writer's arguments come across as clearly as possible. There are no distracting spelling, punctuation, or grammar errors. This keeps the reader right on target.

How to Free Up Free Periods

One of the best ways to learn how to use free time is to have free time to use. At our school, every minute of a student's day is planned out from homeroom to dismissal. The free period isn't free at all since students have to go to study hall or the library during that time.

This is a bad plan. First of all, most kids have been sitting in classes for a few periods before the free period comes up. They need to relax instead of sitting down again.

Second, the study halls are noisy. So even the kids who want to work get distracted by the noise of kids fooling around. On top of that, the study hall monitors spend most of their time yelling at kids to settle down.

Finally, there's the library. Yes, it's quiet there

if you want to work, but is that the best time to get work done? Maybe for some kids it is. But what about kids who prefer to do homework at home? They don't need school time to do their homework.

There are some good reasons to change the present free-period plan to a better one. To begin with, a lot of kids live too far away to see each other except at school. Kids would pay better attention to their later classes if they had a chance to relax beforehand. Most important, there's no better way for kids to learn how to plan their free time than by giving them a little of it.

Maybe people in charge will say that the present plan helps kids who wouldn't do their homework except at school. Even if this is true, is it fair to most of the kids who get their homework done at home?

The school should try out different plans to see how they work out. Maybe just kids with a B+ average or above could get real free periods. Or maybe everyone could get free periods for a month and see what happens. Even one really free period a week would be better than what we have now.

Everybody always says you learn from experience. So give students experience in planning their own free periods.

6
Reporter at Large:
Writing a Research Report

Does the thought of writing a research report make you want to hide until it's over? You are not alone. Many middle school students dread the thought of writing any paper that requires trips to the library, notetaking, and outlines.

Here's what some of them say about this kind of writing project:

"I don't know what to write about."

"I don't know what I'm supposed to copy down at the library."

"Why do I have to use index cards to take notes anyway?"

"I can't find anything good at the library."

"The book I wanted is out."

"How do you get started?"

"I write better at the last minute, and you can't do that with a research paper."

Are these the same worries you have when it comes to writing reports? Does this kind of project seem totally different than the writing you are used to?

Well, here is some good news. You can write a terrific research report following exactly the same ten writing steps you have already learned about. But it's a good idea to brush up on some special library and notetaking skills first.

Using the Library

Before we get into the actual writing steps, let's visit the library first. The *reference section* of your school library or the children's section of your public library are the best places to begin your research. What will you find there for your report?

Encyclopedias can give you background information to get started. But don't depend on them for most of your information. Many teachers discourage students from depending too much on the encyclopedia. You'll enjoy getting information more if you look at simple children's nonfiction books and magazines for background information on your subject.

Atlases contain maps, populations, and facts about places.

Almanacs contain information about statistics. There are hundreds of specialized encyclopedias, almanacs, and atlases.

Nonfiction books are grouped by subjects.

Periodicals include newspapers and magazines. You will use a guide called *The Readers' Guide to Periodical Literature* or a machine called the *Magazine Index* to track down magazines or newspapers about your subject. On the right below is an example of a page from the *Readers' Guide:*

Subject	**Animals**
	See also
	Pets
	Rare animals
	Skin — Animals
	Vision — Animals
	Wildlife
	See also names of animals
Magazine article	Fascinating facts about animals [excerpt from Elephants can't jump] B. Seuling. il *Good Housekeep*
Date of article	201:235 O '85
Author and Magazine	Night of the great circle [tie that binds man and beast] C. K. Warren. il *Read Dig* 127:98–103 N '85

The card catalogue or *microfilm machine* is a collection of cards or entries for every book in the library. Cards for books can be found under titles, authors, or subjects. Most likely you will be using *subject* cards to research your report. Here's what a subject card looks like:

Call number	J 591 L
Subject	ANIMALS
Author	Linsenmaier, Walter
Title	Wonders of Nature
Publishing information	Random House, N.Y., 1979

Plan on two or three trips to the library when you get ready to do your report.

• Make one visit to check out nonfiction books written for younger readers. Writers for younger children highlight the most exciting facts and provide clear illustrations as well. There's no better place to gather background information than a well-written nonfiction children's book. You will find these kinds of books much more fun to read and just as useful as an encyclopedia.

• On a second visit, take out more advanced books on your subject if you need more information.

• If your teacher wants you to do some research in magazines, make a third visit to check the *Readers' Guide* or the *Magazine Index*. Ask the librarian to show you where the magazines you need are kept. Read through the articles and take notes on facts you might want to use in your paper. If you find it hard to write all your notes in the library, make copies of the articles you might want to use later on. Most libraries have a copier for this purpose.

Researching and Notetaking

Notetaking for a research project is different than the kind of notetaking you do in class. Here is what you do:

Keep a large pack of 4″ × 6″ index cards on hand. Fill out a card for each book or magazine article you read. Here is what each of these *bibliography cards* should look like:

Sample Book Card

Author	*Kilpatrick, Cathy*
Title of book	*Creepy Crawlies*
Place of publication	*London, England*
Name of publisher	*Usborne Publishing Ltd.*
Date of publication	*1982*

Sample Magazine Card

Author	*Regis, Edward*
Name of article	*"Dishonest Animals"*
Name of magazine	*OMNI*
Volume number	*Vol. 9 No. 3*
Date of magazine	*December 1986*
Page of article	*p. 43*

Note cards

As you skim books and magazines, you will get a few ideas about how the information is organized. Say you are writing a paper on animal oddities. Some of the information might be about odd-looking animals, strange animal homes, camouflage, strange ways of communicating. These make good headings for individual index cards. As you come across information, write it under the proper heading. Make up new headings as you need them. If you are not sure what headings to use, use some of the chapter titles or index entries from a general book about your subject.

What should you write down? Just facts and quotations followed by the author's last name and the page number of the book or article. All you really need are facts to back up *your* ideas and help you remember where to look back if you need more information. Here is a sample note card. Notice the notes are just a sentence or so:

ODD ANIMAL HOMES
Beavers build safe log canals to get to their lodges. (Mason, P. 54)
Trapdoor spider builds tunnel trap. (Mason, p.64)
Orangutans use palm leaves as blankets at night. (Soule, P. 13)

The library research and the notetaking are the hardest parts of writing a report. The easy part is the actual writing once you have done your research. Why? Because the steps you follow are the same as those you have been following for other kinds of papers.

Now let's see what happens from the time you get the assignment right up to the due date. Chances are your teacher will hand you a set of directions about the report. Whether you get a handout or not, here is what you need to find out before you begin your project:

- When is the report due?
- Do you have to check in with your teacher to see if your topic is acceptable?
- Are you supposed to take notes on note cards?
- Are you required to submit an outline?
- Does your teacher want to see a rough draft?
- How many outside *sources* — books, magazine, or newspaper articles — are you supposed to use?
- What form should the final paper be in? (Does the paper have to have a cover? Should your report include a listing called a bibliography at the end?)

Once you have answered these questions, plan out a schedule. As with other kinds of writing, there are three main stages to schedule: prewriting, writing, revising and editing. Plan one third of the time for each stage. If your paper is due in six weeks, spend two weeks for each section. Remember to schedule a conference early on if your teacher expects to see you at different stages. Set aside time for two or three trips to the library. Use the research paper schedule on pages 84–86 of this book to work out your timetable. A schedule like this helps you break down this big project into easier steps.

To equip yourself for the job, get the following materials together in one place:

- this book
- your research paper schedule
- the teacher's directions
- a dictionary and thesaurus
- 4″ × 6″ lined note cards
- a folder or large envelope to store your work-in-progress
- plenty of lined scrap paper
- several pencils with erasers, a red pencil for corrections, and a pen for your final copy
- an up-to-date library card in your wallet along with some change for the library copier.

Store all this in a shopping or tote bag that you can bring to the library if you plan to do much work there. Research materials have a way of scattering all over the place. Keep it all together in one place to make the job easier.

Now, step-by-step, here's how to plan, research, and write a terrific report:

Assignment: "Write a research report on a subject that interests you."

Prewriting

Step 1: Get personal. You are going to be living with your research subject for several weeks. So it's more important than ever to find a subject you care about. Are you the local expert on racing cars, robots, insects, dinosaurs, ballerinas, mummies, toys, or pets? Do you have a collection of rocks, comic books, seashells, baseball cards, dolls, or weird bottlecaps? Even if your favorite pastime is watching television, then you probably know something about animation, music, trivia, or television heroes.

How do you find a personal subject to write about if you're convinced you aren't an expert in anything? Maybe you enjoy stories about goblins and ghosts. Or you are fascinated by poisonous snakes or other creepy crawlies. Writing a research paper is a great way to learn more about subjects that interest you. Even if you aren't an expert yet, you can become one by writing a research paper on a subject you like.

Step 2: Think small. Many student writers think big instead of small when faced with a research report. A long paper requires a big subject, they think. Not so. Bringing your subject down to a workable size before you even open a book will save you a lot of trouble. Wouldn't you rather read *one* chapter on meat-eating dinosaurs than a *whole* book on dinosaurs? Wouldn't it be easier to learn about the history of the teddy bear than a history of toys?

On the following page are some examples of general subject areas. Below each one is a selection of smaller topics that would lead to a good research report.

Animals:
animal oddities
most deadly animals
famous movie animals
animal language
almost-extinct animals
animals that made a comeback
top ten dog breeds
animals that saved people's lives
Eskimo sled dogs

Supernatural:
famous haunted houses
ghosts in the movies
UFO's in the last five years
Bigfoot and other monster legends
the facts about the Bermuda triangle
alien contact: fact or fiction

Mystery and Crime:
famous unsolved crimes
great escapes
famous spies
outlaws of the Old West
famous robberies
famous disappearances

If you have trouble getting your subject down to a workable size, see your teacher right away or talk to one of your parents. Sometimes just talking about a subject helps you discover just the angle you need to manage your subject. You can also go to the card catalogue and flip through the cards on your general subject. You may get good report ideas from just reading book titles.

There are hundreds of reference books in your library where you might get ideas. Browse through some of them and see if you turn up any good writing ideas.

Step 3: Make a list. Remember how you listed all your ideas for other kinds of papers? In those papers, most of the items on your list came from your head. In a research paper, most of the information will come from your sources. *Sources* are the books, magazines, newspapers, surveys, and interviews you will use to get information.

But before you set foot in the library, spend fifteen minutes or so writing down every idea of your own that pops into your head when you think of your topic. You probably know more than you think already. And your ideas are the best *sources* for any paper. Trust in your own point of view when you start out. Save the outside experts for later on.

Once you have listed your own thoughts, it's time to get to the library. Schedule your first visit as early as possible to get first crack at the materials you might need. Most teachers teach library skills right around the time they assign a research report.

But if you are on your own, you will need special help from a librarian. Here's what to do:

On your first library visit, introduce yourself to the librarian. School and children's librarians are used to helping students with research papers. Tell the librarian that you want to find some children's books on your subject. The librarian will probably bring you to the subject section of the card catalogue where you can find general subjects like animals, cars, dancers, stamps. If a book looks good, copy down the call number, title, and last name of the author. Then get the books from the shelves, check them out, and bring them home.

Spend a week or so skimming the books. Carefully read the sections that tie into your subject. Take notes on note cards as you read. Remember, just write down facts and quotations to save time. Write out a bibliography card for every book you read.

On your next trip to the library, you might want to get out more advanced books on your subject.

Your last trip to the library should be to check on magazines and oddball reference books.

Ask the librarian to show you how to use *The Readers' Guide to Periodical Literature*. Look up your general subject, say *animal* or *volcanoes*. Then check any smaller topics underneath that tie in with your subject. Copy down the information and ask the librarian to show you where you can find the magazines or newspapers. On an index card, write down any facts or quotations you might want to use later on. Then make up a bibliography card like the one shown earlier in this chapter.

When you think you have plenty of information for your report, you can move on to:

Step 4: Organize. Now you will see why you have been taking your notes on cards rather than on sheets of paper. Gather your pile of note cards along with your own list of ideas. Lay your note cards out on a table and read them over.

Do you begin to see a way to put them in order? Are you getting some ideas about the purpose of your paper? What you are looking for as you look over your notes is some big idea that will tie together most of the information. A set of note cards about animal oddities might make you realize that animals protect themselves in strange ways. This is called the *main idea* or *thesis statement*.

Sometimes a writer looks over a set of notes and doesn't see a main idea right away. This might happen to you. If it does, see your teacher. Most teachers expect to be consulted as students work on their reports. Bring along your note cards and ask for help in coming up with a main idea. Or ask a parent to help you go over the cards.

Once you have a main idea, arrange your note cards in the order you plan to use them. Then work on your outline. Each heading you want to use from your note cards should become an entry on the outline. In other words, you get the information for an outline from your note cards.

Here is a sample of how to begin a research report outline:

OUTLINE

Your name: _____
Date: _____
Topic: Animal oddities

Main Idea: Animals protect themselves in very strange ways.

Introduction: (Write down some of your own ideas about what you think you are going to say in the rest of the paper.)

I. Animal homes
   A. Mammal homes
      1. Beaver and platypus lodges
      2. Gorilla nests
   B. Bird homes
      1. Weaver birds
      2. Baltimore oriole's trapeze nest
   C. Insect/spider homes
      1. Trapdoor spider tunnels
      2. Mud dauber wasp

II. Camouflage
    A. Green tree frog
    B. Bittern bird
    C. Lantern fly

Conclusion: (Write down a summary of how you plan to end your paper. Remember, your outline is just a guide to get you started. You can always change any part of the actual paper later on.)

The entries on your outline should match the headings on your note cards. If you have six note card headings, you should have six outline entries to write after the Roman numerals. We have just shown two entries in this outline. Most research papers will have more.

Once you complete your outline, you are ready to move on to:

Writing
Step 5: Introduce. This should go smoothly since you already have a main idea. In a research report you will need to write a longer introduction to get across what you are going to say. Here's an example:

Animals have very strange ways of protecting themselves. Some animals build unusual homes in which they can hide from their enemies. Others are born with camouflage that hides them from enemies. There are animals that make strange sounds to imitate other creatures in order to protect themselves. Some animals have odd habits that help them hide from their enemies. The animal kingdom is full of oddities that help different kinds of animals stay alive.

With an opener like this, the writer can then move on to develop each of the headings in the outline.

Step 6: Develop. The writer has done a good job of setting up each of the areas to be lengthened later on. In each paragraph, the writer will then make a statement about the headings like strange homes, camouflage, etc., then back it up with examples, facts, or experts' quotations from the note cards.

After each point is developed, the writer is ready to sum up.

Step 7: Write your ending. Remember that the ending should tie up all the different parts of the paper and repeat the main idea in a new way. Here's an example:

Nature is full of surprises. Animal homes, camouflage, and odd animal habits and features all help animals stay alive. Some animals seem odd, but there is a good reason for their oddities: protecting themselves.

Step 8: Think of a title. Here are several possibilities:

- *Animal Oddities*
- *Wonders of the Animal World*
- *How Odd: Strange Creatures*
- *Creature Features: Animal Oddities*

If you use a funny title, put a colon after it, then follow with a straightforward subtitle as in the last example. It's important for your reader to know the subject right away.

Revising and Editing

Once you have a rough draft, follow Steps 9 and 10 — revising, editing, and recopying — just as you have in other kinds of writing. When revising a research report, be sure you back up any opinion you have with some fact from your research. If you use an expert's opinion, be sure to mention the person's name and put quotations around what he or she said.

Bibliography Page

If your teacher requires a bibliography page, arrange your bibliography cards in alphabetical order. Then copy the information on a sheet like this:

BIBLIOGRAPHY

(author) Daly, Kathleen. (title) Unusual Animals. (City of Publication) New York: (Publisher) Golden Press, (Year) 1977.

Hess, Lilo. Animals That Hide, Imitate and Bluff. New York: Charles Scribner's Sons, 1970.

Kilpatrick, Cathy. Creepy Crawlers. London, England: Usborne Press Ltd., 1982.

Linsenmaier, Walter. Wonders of Nature. New York: Random House, 1979.

McClung, Robert M. How Animals Hide. Washington, D.C.: National Geographic Society, 1973.

Mason, George F. Animal Homes. New York: William Morrow Company, 1947.

Roth, Charles E. Walking Catfish and Other Aliens. Reading, Massachusetts: Addison-Wesley, 1973.

Soule, Gardner. Strange Things Animals Do. New York: G. P. Putnam's Sons, 1970.

MAGAZINE ARTICLES

Regis, Edward, Jr. "Dishonest Animals." OMNI, December 1986, p. 43.

Warner, David. "Ask an Armadillo." Ranger Rick, July 1986, pp. 33–37.

Turning In Your Research Report

Gather everything your teacher said to turn in. Many teachers want to see your note cards, bibliography cards, outline, and rough draft along with your final copy. If you are required to submit your paper inside a cover or with a title page, make sure you do that.

A research report is a lot of work. But if you follow each step carefully, you will write a report you can be proud of.

Here are some real tips from older students who have written research reports and lived to tell about it:

"Try to tell a story with your paper. I once wrote a research report about a day in the life of a skunk."

"Pretend your paper is an educational TV show and you're the narrator. Use information a person can picture, not just a bunch of numbers."

"At first, doing index cards is a pain. But once you figure it out, it makes a lot of sense because you can shuffle them in the order you want."

"One of my teachers said we could interview people or make up questionnaires for our research. So I did a paper on fast food and asked my friends about whether they like McDonald's or Burger King better."

"Once I had so many notes, I didn't know what to do

with them. So I wrote my rough draft without any notes, then fit stuff in later on. The paper turned out great anyway!"

"Don't be afraid to ask people for help along the way. I saw my teacher three times before I finished my last report. And I talked to the librarian, too."

"One great thing about turning in a research paper: You don't have to do another one until next year!"

7
A Writer's Survival Kit

Checklist: 10 Steps to A+ Writing

Prewriting

Step 1. Get personal. Pick a subject you know about or personalize an assigned subject. (Question: What experiences from my life can I tie into this writing assignment?)

Step 2. Think small. Narrow your subject down to a workable size. (Question: What part of this subject interests me most?)

Step 3. Make a list. List all the specific details you can think of about your topic. (Question: When I close my eyes, what specific details do I picture that will *show* the reader what I want to say?)

Step 4. Organize. Decide on a plan and purpose for your paper. (Question: What is the best way to arrange my list?)

Writing

Step 5. Introduce. Write the opening sentence. (Question: What do I want the reader to know right away?)

Step 6. Develop. Write the supporting paragraphs that develop the main ideas from your planning list. (Question: Which supporting ideas tie into my main one?)

Step 7. Write your ending. (Question: How can I repeat my main idea in a new way?)

Step 8. Think of a title. (Question: How can I make a good first impression with the title?)

Revising and Editing

Step 9. Revise. (Question: How can I improve the style of what I have written?)

Step 10. Edit and recopy. (Question: Is everything as correct as I can make it?)

Outline Form

Main Idea: _____ .

_____

_____

Introduction: _____

_____

_____

I. _____

    A. _____

        1. _____

        2. _____

    B. _____

        1. _____

        2. _____

    C. _____

        1. _____

        2. _____

II. _____

    A. _____

        1. _____

        2. _____

    B. _____

        1. _____

        2. _____

    C. _____

        1. _____

        2. _____

III. _____

    A. _____

        1. _____

        2. _____

    B. _____

        1. _____

        2. _____

C. _____
   1. _____
   2. _____

Conclusion: _____

Research Paper Schedule

Research
Jobs to be done:

	Due Dates:	Check-off:
1. Think of a general subject that interests you.	_____	_____
2. Narrow your general subject down to a specific subtopic.	_____	_____
3. Go to the library for information on your topic. Make a list of all usable research sources on bibliography cards.	_____	_____
4. Take notes on the materials you listed. Record your research on note cards.	_____	_____
5. Write a thesis statement that sums up the main point of your paper and the research you have uncovered so far.	_____	_____

Organizing Your Paper

6. Read over your note cards   _____   _____
   and decide which informa-
   tion to include or omit.

7. Arrange your note cards in   _____   _____
   logical order.

8. Write an outline based on   _____   _____
   the arrangement of your
   note cards.

Writing Your Paper

9. Write a rough draft of your   _____   _____
   paper, main point by main
   point, from your outline
   and note cards. Support
   each main idea with facts,
   examples, and subtopics
   from your note cards.

10. Work on the introduction   _____   _____
    and conclusion.

11. Go over your rough draft   _____   _____
    to see if all your ideas re-
    late to one another and to
    your main idea. Check that
    you've supported all your
    main ideas with researched
    facts and examples. Polish
    the style of your rough
    draft.

Writing Your Paper

12. Rewrite your rough draft   _____   _____
    into a final copy. Docu-
    ment facts, quotations, and
    passages with footnotes.
    Write up a bibliography
    sheet from your bibliog-
    raphy cards.

13. Proofread your final draft   _____   _____
    for mechanics and neat-
    ness.

14. Submit your paper on the   _____   _____
    due date.

Revising Sheet

Yes No Organization:

☐ ☐ Does my main idea come across right
away?

☐ ☐ Does each paragraph tie in with my main
idea?

☐ ☐ Does the order make sense?

☐ ☐ Does my last paragraph get my main idea
across in a new, interesting way?

☐ ☐ Did I include everything?

☐ ☐ Are there parts I should leave out?

Yes No Style:

☐ ☐ I have used very specific words.

☐ ☐ I have used different kinds of sentence patterns.

☐ ☐ I have shifted smoothly from one paragraph to the next.

☐ ☐ I have tied up all my ideas at the end.

Editing Sheet

Yes No Grammar, Spelling, Punctuation

☐ ☐ I have written my name, the date, and title on my paper.

☐ ☐ I began each sentence with a capital letter.

☐ ☐ I put a period, question mark, or exclamation point at the end of each sentence.

☐ ☐ I put a comma where I paused between ideas in a sentence.

☐ ☐ I left a few spaces before starting each paragraph.

☐ ☐ I spelled each word correctly.

☐ ☐ I put conversations inside quotation marks.

Proofreading Sheet

Use these signs to make corrections on your rough draft as you read it out loud.

$\wedge$ This arrow shows where⁀add

      a word, phrase, or punctuation mark.

$\equiv$ capitalize the word.

⌗ ⌗Start a new paragraph.

⟋   Take out the extra word or or words.

$\cap$ Reverse the lettres.

/   Split the words that are jammed together.

⊙   Add a period⊙

⤸   Move this to a better place. (If you have a whole paragraph to move, you may want to cut apart your paper and rearrange and tape it in a better order. You can save time doing this instead of recopying everything just to see how the new arrangement looks.)

ˇˇ ˇˇ ˇˇ Add quotation marks, she said. ˇˇ

88

Easy Reference Grammar Sheet

Grammar Definitions

A sentence is a group of words that says a complete thought. A sentence has two parts: the *subject*, or noun part, names what the sentence is about. The *predicate*, or verb part, tells what the subject is doing.

A sentence begins with a capital letter and ends with a period, question mark, or exclamation point.

> **Sentence:** The window in the attic was closed.
> **Not a sentence:** the window in the attic

A paragraph is a group of sentences about one idea. Indent, or start, a new paragraph a few spaces in every time you shift scenes or begin a new idea.

Punctuation Rules

Period (.) Use a period after any sentence that makes a statement:

> The car needs to be washed.

Use a period after abbreviations of names, places, and months:

> Mr., Dr., N.Y., Jan.

Question mark (?) Use a question mark after a question or parts in a series of questions:

> What are you eating? Fish? Meat? Eggs?

Exclamation point (!)   Use an exclamation point after a sentence that expresses strong feelings.

We won!

Comma (,)   Use a comma to indicate pauses you make when you read your paper out loud. Here are examples showing the most common use of commas:

I ride the bus on Monday, Tuesday, and Wednesday.
She lives in Los Angeles, California.
No, I'm busy Friday night.
Naomi, a flute player, joined the orchestra.
Although I don't feel well, I still want to go.
"Let's work on this together," Bill suggested.
May 23, 1962
The lights flickered, and the electricity went out.

Colon (:)   Use the colon to introduce a list of items, after the salutation of a business letter, or before a famous quotation:

Write on the list: batteries, hooks, nails.
Dear Sir:
I know just what Harry Truman meant when he said: "The buck stops here."

Semicolon (;)   Use the semicolon to separate

two thoughts that could have been connected by *and, but, or:*

The highway was backed up; we took a detour instead.

Use a semicolon to separate series of words that have commas within them:

Breakfast consists of grapefruit, oranges, or fruit cup; oatmeal, corn flakes, or bran; eggs, pancakes, or waffles.

Quotation marks (" ")   Use quotation marks to indicate a person's conversation.

He asked, "What time does the train leave?"

Indicate titles of articles, short stories, poems, songs, with quotation marks.

I sing "The Star-Spangled Banner."

Underline titles indicating full-length books, musicals, programs, magazines, newspapers, etc.

The Daily News, Newsweek, Cats.

Commas and periods *always* go *inside* quotation marks.

"I'm leaving now," she said, "but I'll be back."

Colons and semicolons go outside the quotation marks.

I was told, "Leave the lights on when you go"; I don't know why.

Question marks and exclamation points go *inside* the marks if the material quoted is a question or exclamation.

"Watch out!" Henry warned.

If the quoted material is not a question or exclamation, but the rest of the sentence is, the marks go *outside*.

Does your doctor always say, "An apple a day keeps the doctor away"?

Apostrophe (')   Use an apostrophe to show possession. Add an apostrophe and an "s" on a singular word.

Bob's car.

After a plural, add the apostrophe *after* the "s."

The girls' hockey sticks were missing.

If the plural doesn't end in "s," put the apostrophe before the "s."

Women's Room

An apostrophe also indicates a missing letter.

isn't, aren't

Use an apostrophe to indicate the plural of numbers and letters.

How many C's did you get on your report card?

100 Writing Topics

Topics You Can Write About in One Paragraph

1. Describe yourself in one sentence, then write several supporting sentences that show examples of what you said.
2. Tell about a recent dream you remember.
3. In one paragraph, convince somebody to read a book you read or see a movie you liked. Give your opinion in the first sentence and follow up with supporting examples from the book or movie.
4. In one paragraph, make the reader's mouth water by describing the reasons you love a certain snack or food.
5. In a paragraph, write down five things you think of when you hear the word "summer."
6. Describe how you get ready for bed.
7. Describe the typical first fifteen minutes when you wake up on a school day.
8. In a paragraph, tell a recent joke that made you laugh.
9. Tell how you broke a bad habit.
10. If you didn't have to write this paragraph, tell what you would do with the time instead.

Writing a Personal Narrative

11. Describe a dream day you would like to have on your next birthday.

12. Describe what it would be like to be invisible for a day.
13. If you had stayed home from school today, what would your day have been like?
14. If you could be in a time machine today, what would your day be like?
15. Describe your most recent visit to the dentist.
16. Describe a memorable day you had recently.
17–21. Write about a day in the life of one of the following objects as if you *were* that object: a toothbrush, a dollar bill, a pencil, a sneaker, a bookbag.
22. Make up a plot for your favorite television show and summarize it.
23. Describe a memorable first day of school.
24. If you were allowed to stay up one hour later every night and could do exactly what you wanted with that extra hour, what would you do with the time? (Imagine you could use that extra hour any time of day.)
25. Remember when you lost something very important and your feelings while the object was still lost. Then describe the moments of finding the object and the feelings you had then.
26. Describe what your life would be like if school time and vacation times were reversed. That is, you would go to school during the times you now have vacations and have vacations when you now go to school.

27–30. Compare and contrast what a day in your life would be like if you could live it as: one of your parents; someone you would secretly like to be; your teacher; your pet.

Writing a Description

31. Take a fifteen-minute walk someplace and bring a notepad along. At the end of fifteen minutes write down what you noticed along the way, then write a description of what you saw.

32. Describe a favorite holiday from beginning to end.

33. Write about something from memory, in as much detail as possible. Then go look at the object and write about it as it appears in front of you.

34–41. Compare: two houses or apartments you've lived in; two schools or grades you were in; two vacation spots you've visited; two friends you have; two books by the same author; two kinds of fast foods; two birthday parties you've had or been to; two bedrooms you've had.

42. Compare the advantages and disadvantages of two different seasons.

43. If you are a girl, describe what you think your life would be like if you were a boy; if you're a boy, describe what your life would be like if you were a girl.

44. Describe what exactly makes you happy.
45. Describe how a certain kind of day affects your mood.
46. Describe what gives you a sense of pride and accomplishment.
47–51. Use this beginning in a paper: "When I hear the word ——— , I think of ——— ." Possible words to write about: "gym," "water," "camp," "school bus," "snow."

Writing a How-to Paper
52. Explain how you solved a personal problem.
53. Explain how you broke a bad habit or started a good one.
54. Explain the rules of a favorite game in such a way that a person who never played it could start, after reading your directions.
55. Explain how you got over a fear you once had.
56. Describe how you do a particular chore at home or manage all your chores. Write your paper as if you were leaving directions for someone else to do the job.
57. Explain how to tie a shoe.
58. Write up directions to your house for someone walking from a mile away. Make sure you describe scenes and landmarks to look for along the way.
59. Write a description of how to shop for, prepare, and serve your favorite meal.

60. Explain the steps in teaching your pet a trick.

61–65. Describe your personal method for eating one of the following foods: an Oreo cookie, a plate of spaghetti, an ice cream cone, corn on the cob, or a hot dog.

Writing a Personal Opinion

66. Imagine that you are a parent of a child who is your age. Discuss which family rules you would change for your own child and which you would keep.

67. Describe what you like and dislike about being the age you are.

68. Write about whether you think kids your age should (or should not) be paid for getting good grades.

69. Write your opinion about whether kids your age should be allowed to set their own bedtimes.

70. Write about whether kids your age should be given a clothing allowance to buy whatever clothes they want.

71. Write a note to your parents giving reasons your allowance should be increased by a certain amount.

72. Write a note to your parents in which you try to convince them to allow you to do something you are not now allowed to do.

73. Write a note to your school principal giving good reasons for kids in your grade to be allowed to do something they can't do now.
74. Write a paper that begins with the line: "Don't waste your money (or time) on ———— ."
75. Describe what you would put in a time capsule the size of a one-foot square carton that would be opened in the year 2050 by a grandchild who will be your current age. Give reasons for your choices.
76. Describe what makes a good friend.

Wishful Thinking

77. If you could be granted one wish, what would you do with it?
78. If you could change one thing in your life, what would it be?
79. What name would you choose if you could change your name?
80. If your pet could talk, what would it say?
81. If a dream you had while sleeping could come true, which dream would you pick?
82. If you found a hundred dollars today and could keep it, what would you do with the money?
83. If you could change the age you are, which age would you most like to be?
84. If you had to leave your house in a hurry and could only take one thing, what would it be?

85. If you could invite anyone over for the weekend, who would you invite?
86. If you could change one of your physical features, which would it be?
87. If you knew you would live one year longer if you never ate another piece of candy, would you be willing to give up candy?
88. Imagine you are the winner of a gift certificate to your favorite store. The prize? A ten-minute shopping spree in which you could select anything in the store. Write a paper describing the store you would pick and what you would plan to get.

Just for Openers

The more often you follow the writing steps suggested in this book, the more automatic the steps will become, no matter what kind of paper you want to write. But every once in a while, no matter what you do, you may not be able to gather enough ideas for a paper or figure out a plan for writing one. Sometimes what you need is just one line to get started. Here are several first lines to get those juices flowing:

89. *Crash!*
90. I really knew I was in big trouble when . . .
91. If there's one thing I just can't stand it's . . .
92. If I knew what kind of day it was going to be, I never would have gotten out of bed.

93. Sometimes a person just has to learn things the hard way.
94. Sometimes being a kid isn't what it's cracked up to be.

Last Words

See if you can come up with a paper that builds up to one of these closing sentences:

95. If someone else can come up with a better explanation, I sure would like to hear it!
96. I saw it with my own eyes!
97. Sure, there were a lot of other things I could have done, but sometimes you only get one chance.
98. Nobody said it was going to be easy, and it wasn't!
99. The day ended the way it began, with the sound of a howling animal in the distance.
100. When I woke up, I realized where I was — back in my own room again.

Writer's Scorecard

Keep track of your strengths and weaknesses in writing. Each time you get back a corrected paper, write the title, date, and grade in the columns shown on page 103. Then, in a phrase or two, write in what the teacher considered to be your strong and weak points in the paper. Before you write your next assignment, check over your strong points and weak points to see what you can build on or correct. Whether you use this scorecard or not, do save all your papers in a folder so you can get a sense of how you are progressing as a writer. They might be valuable someday!

Title	Date	Strong Points	Weak Points

INDEX

Almanacs, 62
Apostrophe, 92-93
Arguments. *See* Persuasive writing.
Atlases, 62

Bibliography, 64-65, 72, 73, 77-78, 84, 86
Books, nonfiction. 62-63, 64. *See also* Reference books.

Card catalogue, 62-63, 71, 72
Colon, 90, 92
Comma, 90, 91
Compare/contrast, 52, 53
Conclusion, 11-12, 82, 101
   of descriptions, 37
   of explanations, 46
   of personal narratives, 26
   of persuasive writing, 57
   of research reports, 75, 76, 85

Description, 30-39, 96-97
Details, 7-9
   for descriptions, 33-34
   for expository writing, 43
   for personal narratives, 20-23
   for persuasive writing, 51-52, 53
Development, 10-11, 82
   of descriptions, 35-36
   of expository writing, 44-46
   of personal narratives, 24-26
   of persuasive writing, 55-57
   of research reports, 76